The Georgia Guide to Quirky Questions

Written by Jacqueline Leigh   Illustrated by Maya Gur

PELICAN PUBLISHING
NEW ORLEANS

For all the curious people. I encourage you to celebrate your differences and wear your uniqueness proudly.
—J. L.

To Liya and Tamara, my curious girls, and all the curious kids around the world, for the questions you will freely ask and the colorful answers you will find
—With love, Maya

The word "Pelican" and the depiction of a pelican are trademarks of Arcadia Publishing Company Inc. and are registered in the U.S. Patent and Trademark Office.

Library of Congress Cataloging-in-Publication Data

Names: Leigh, Jacqueline, author. | Gur, Maya, illustrator.
Title: The Georgia guide to quirky questions / Written by Jacqueline Leigh; Illustrated by Maya Gur.
Description: New Orleans : Pelican Publishing, [2023] | Summary: "You get to go on a field trip! Do you want to taste Coke at the World of Coca-Cola or stargaze at the Fernbank Science Center? This picture book of quirky questions spurs Georgia youngsters to express their individuality."— Provided by publisher.
Identifiers: LCCN 2022035051 | ISBN 9781455626861 (hardback) | ISBN 9781455626878 (ebook)
Subjects: LCSH: Individuality in children—Juvenile literature. | Georgia—Description and travel—Juvenile literature. | Questions and answers—Juvenile literature.
Classification: LCC LB1083 .L44 2023 | DDC 370.15/32—dc23/eng/20220805
LC record available at https://lccn.loc.gov/2022035051

Printed in Korea
Published by Pelican Publishing
New Orleans, LA
www.pelicanpub.com

Introduction

Just like the flowers on a dogwood and the fuzz of a peach, we are all different in our own way.

Some of us might look the same or talk alike, but that doesn't mean we are the same. We might share beliefs or even have similar quirks, but we are still different. Our differences—even small ones—make us unique.

What are some of these differences? The sometimes silly and always curious questions that follow will help you understand those differences. Keep in mind, there are no right or wrong answers, just answers that will make you laugh, smile, and learn a little something new about yourself.

Let's Go to School!

Have you ever dreamed of being a scientist, a veterinarian, or a pilot? Dreaming of a successful career is half the fun of being a kid. Luckily, we have a wonderful place that helps us become what we dream—school.

Yes, days can be long, pencils can break, and textbooks are heavy, but don't let that fool you. Teachers fill your brains with important stuff.

Some of it is fun, like making volcanoes and going on field trips. Some of it is hard, like solving math problems and writing essays. When it gets hard, raise your hand and ask questions.

We learn and grow by asking questions.

Speaking of questions, the bell just rang. Take your seats and listen up.

Questions:

Some people take cars, some ride the school bus, in the big city they take MARTA and in Peachtree City they drive golf carts. What form of transportation would you most like to take to school and back?

What is your dream job?

It's lunchtime. Who do you want to sit next to in the cafeteria?

If you could get rid of one subject in school, what would it be?

Your teacher wants you to read out loud in front of the class. Are you:
a) excited to share how well you read,
b) a little bit nervous,
c) scared and shy or
d) you escape to the restroom!

Which of your classmates is most likely to become a comedian?

At recess, what playground equipment do you run to first?

What is your favorite playground game?

You get to go on a field trip!
Do you want to taste Coke at the
World of Coca-Cola or star gaze at
the Fernbank Science Center?

What's the nicest thing your teacher has ever said to you?

What is your favorite item of clothing to wear to school?

Do you miss anyone when you're at school?

What is your all-time favorite show & tell item?

What's the hardest rule to follow at school?

Which friend would you love to work on a
school project with?

Would you rather be an
artist at the Savannah
College of Art and Design
or a computer whiz at
Georgia Tech?

Let's Go to the Georgia National Fair in Perry!

Have you ever heard someone say, "Life is like a roller coaster?"

This phrase means that life is full of ups and downs, sad moments and happy moments, sunny days and rainy days.

Sometimes, life feels like a Ferris wheel. It goes around and around and around, and you see the same people, do the same things and eat the same food every day.

Sometimes, life is more like riding in a bumper car. You are in the driver's seat, and you get to decide where you go and how fast or how slow. But sometimes you get pushed in a lot of different directions!

For now, please keep your hands and feet inside the ride. We are heading to the Georgia National Fair in Perry!

Questions:

You have to enter an eating contest. Do you enter the fried chicken contest or the peach cobbler contest?

You just won the ring toss!
Do you choose:
a) the cuddly stuffed animal,
b) the monster water gun,
c) the oversized sunglasses or
d) The old balloon with the leak?

Which ride do you prefer, the Ferris wheel or the bumper cars?

What is your favorite fair food?

Do you like to go to the fair first thing in the morning to get the best spot in line or at night when you get to see the pretty lights?

If you won a goldfish, what would you name it?

What TV show character would you pick to sit next to on the roller coaster?

Someone cuts
in front of you
in the ride line.
What do you do?

If you had
to work at the fair,
what job would you choose?

Dancing on stage at the fair is a popular
event. What song would you dance to?

What kind of facial expression do
you make in the photo booth?

At the beauty pageant,
what does the winner look like?

Would you rather be thrown
from a bull at the rodeo
or stuck at the top of the
Ferris wheel?

Let's Go to Centennial Olympic Park in Atlanta!

Centennial Olympic Park is in the heart of Atlanta and is full of outdoor fun. Even if you don't live near this big city park, you likely have terrific local parks in your hometown.

Speeding across the monkey bars, gazing at a beautiful magnolia tree, or freeze-tagging your best buddies are just three outdoor activities we love.

Playing outside makes us stronger, soaking up the sun helps us feel happier, and time away from electronics clears our minds.

Quick—run outside and straight into these beaming questions!

Questions:

You have to do one chore before you can go to the park. Pick that chore!

What would you do if you saw a snake slithering down the slide?

Would you rather be able to climb the monkey bars backward or do a backflip off them?

Oh, look, a field of your favorite flowers! What flowers are they?

You can only take one item with you to the park. What do you take?

What adult in your life would have the most fun playing at a park?

If you saw someone your age playing alone on the swing set, would you:
a) Start swinging next to this person,
b) Invite this person to play with you,
c) Wave and continue doing your own activity or
d) Hide behind the seesaw?

Oh yum! You packed a picnic to eat. What's in your picnic basket?

What playground skill do you wish you were really good at?

How would it make you feel if you saw a rainbow?

There are two superheroes on the seesaw. Who are they?

It's Earth Day, a day when we all pitch in to help
keep our planet clean. How would you like to help:
a) by walking to the park instead of taking the car,
b) by planting a tree,
c) by picking up trash or
d) by chasing butterflies?

What is your favorite memory of you
and your family or friends at a park?

Well I Declare, Let's Celebrate!

Celebrating makes us feel good, whether we're trick or treating on Halloween, making a card for someone special on Valentine's Day, or staying up late for fireworks on the Fourth of July.

Do you know what a tradition is? It's when you do something over and over again, every single year. Maybe you eat turkey every year at Thanksgiving. That's a tradition. Maybe you read a special book every Christmas Eve. That's a tradition. Maybe you make a special treat for someone you love on their birthday. That's a tradition. Traditions are a great way for family and friends to come together year after year.

Speaking of traditions, please pass the hash brown casserole. Let's sit around the table and chat about the holidays!

Questions:

What is your favorite holiday tradition?

What will you be next year for Halloween?

If it could be one holiday every single day of the year, what holiday would you choose?

Do you join the carolers around town or decorate the town Christmas tree?

There are six chairs at the Thanksgiving dinner table. Who is sitting in those chairs?

Would you rather open Christmas presents blindfolded, make Valentine's blindfolded or eat Halloween candy blindfolded?

You get to have dinner with the Easter Bunny.
Where do you go?

Valentine's Day is all about love.
What can you do to show your love?

You ran out of milk and cookies on Christmas Eve.
What will you leave out for Santa?

You have to pick just one person to watch the Fourth of
July fireworks with. Who do you pick?

All of the houses are giving out the same candy on
Halloween. What candy do you hope to receive?

If you could make up your own holiday,
what would it be called?

A new year, a new you! What would you like to change
or improve about yourself in the new year?

What's your favorite Thanksgiving dish?

Let's Visit Your Local Swimming Hole!

You slip into your favorite bathing suit and grab a colorful towel. Sunglasses hide your eyes, and sunscreen covers your face. You jump in the car, roll down the windows, and take off.

Whether your swimming spot is a pool, a vast ocean, a quiet lake, or even a shallow river, swimming is one of the most relaxing activities you can enjoy. When you feel stressed or anxious, make a plan to go swimming. Just make sure you've had lessons first!

After even thirty minutes in the water, you will leave feeling happier than when you arrived. Whether you prefer diving for toys, lounging on a float, or cannon-balling off a dock, swimming is a great way to relax and have a good time.

Questions:

Which do you prefer to swim in, a lake, a pool, or the ocean?

Would you rather build sandcastles, fly a kite or hunt for seashells?

You've been invited to a pool birthday party. What gift do you bring?

Describe your perfect swimming day. Where are you? Who are you with?

You're at the lake, and you get to do the weather report for the local news. What water creature is your co-host? What's the weather like today?

You can either dance in the waterfall at Toccoa Falls or jump the waves at Tybee Island, which sounds more exciting?

Three fun activities have been planned at the same time. Which activity do you choose?
a) swimming with the dolphins,
b) deep-sea fishing or
c) surfing lessons?

What does your sandcastle look like?

You are taking a walk on the beach when,
all of a sudden, you see the most amazing thing.
What is it?

What does it sound like when ocean creatures
speak to each other?

You are racing at a swim meet. What positive phrase
do you say to yourself right before the race starts?

Would you rather go night swimming in a pool
or catch crabs at night on the beach?

Camping at the lake is fun! What story will
you share around the bonfire?

What's the best and worst
swimming snack?

Let's Go on a Trip!

We live in a giant world filled with adventures. It's exciting to pack our bags, grab our cameras, and load our cars.

Whether we're traveling two miles or two thousand, whether we're going to the beach, the mountains, or a big city beaming with lights, traveling provides new experiences. We meet new people, eat new foods, and learn new things. We often get to sleep a little later, take a break from our daily routines, and make special memories that we might not have the opportunity to create at home.

Let's make some memories right now! Pack your bags and adventure into these questions.

Questions:

Let's take a trip. Where should we go?

How do you get there?

You can only bring one suitcase. What do you pack?

What is your favorite road trip snack?

Would you rather go tubing in Helen, Georgia or see the wild horses on Cumberland Island?

What is your favorite thing about staying in a hotel?

Would you rather ride on an airplane or take the train?

What road trip game do you like to play?

You get to meet one celebrity on your trip.
Would you pick:
a) the President of the United States,
b) your favorite musician,
c) an Olympic gold medalist or
d The bulldog that just won the
       "most slobbery dog contest?"

How do you relax on vacation?

Who do you want to bunk with in the hotel room?

You're in charge of taking pictures.
What do you take pictures of?

At the end of your trip, are you excited
or sad to go home?

Let's Go to the Macon State Farmers Market!

Peanuts, watermelon, and tomatoes are just a few of the nutritious foods we can find at the market. These fresh foods can help us stay healthy, help our brains hold more information, and help us get a good night's sleep.

After you stock up on healthy items from the local farmer's, don't forget to have a little fun. After all, I scream, you scream, we all scream for ice cream.

Head over to Farmer Buck's fruit stand to answer some fun questions!

Questions:

Do you need a large wagon or a small basket
for your trip?

Do you prefer spicy foods or sour foods?

If you could sample two items at the market,
what would they be?

Uh-oh, someone made a big mess, what food would
you not want to clean up?

What items do you need to make your
favorite food?

Would you rather buy junk food
or healthy food?

How many bags of boiled peanuts can you eat?

You get one food item free for the rest of your life! What one item do you want?

You have to buy food for your school lunch. What do you buy?

You time-traveled back 100 years. What do you see at the market?

If you get to have a sleepover in the market, what booth would you sleep in?

What food have you never tried before that you want to try?

What famous person or character would you like to eat dessert with?

You're being put to work at the market, do you want to:
a) peel the layers of a Vidalia onion
b) bottle barbecue sauce, or
c) crack peanut shells?

Let's Go to Zoo Atlanta!

Did you know that giraffes are among the most graceful animals in the world? That lions are among the strongest? That bears are among the most affectionate? That monkeys are among the smartest?

Hearing this might be surprising. That's why it's important not to judge people or animals by the way they look. We can learn a lot from animals, and visiting them at the zoo is one of the best ways to do this.

Are you as graceful as a giraffe? As strong as a lion? As affectionate as a bear? As smart as a monkey? Let's take a look at the questions below and see if your animal instincts kick in.

Questions:

If you could take an animal home from the zoo, what animal would you choose?

You accidentally fell into the monkey cage. What do you do?

Which animal is most like you?

In a game of hide and seek, which animal would win?

An elephant escaped! How will you get him back to his exhibit?

Would you rather ride on the back of a bear or the back of a gorilla?

If a flamingo had a superpower, what would it be?

What do giraffes dream about?

If you could, what two zoo animals would you combine?

You get to be the zoo trainer for the day.
What cool tricks will you teach the lions?

What is your least favorite animal at the zoo?

There's an animal race!
Which animal will you root for?
a) the cheetah,
b) the ostrich,
c) the wild dog or
d) the sloth?

You are walking through the birdhouse exhibit.
What is your best bird call?

What animal makes you laugh the most?

Let's Go Home, Y'all!

"Home" is a very important word. Your home is a shelter from bad weather and bad days. It's a safe place to laugh, cry, smile, yell, rest, and play.

Some homes are tucked away in the woods, some are nestled close to their neighbors, and some are in buildings that touch the sky. No matter where your house sits, it's a place to call home.

After a long day at school, work, or running errands, you get to go home. You might toss your backpack in the corner, kick your shoes off, and grab your favorite snack. This is your space to be uniquely you.

Welcome home!

Questions:

What room in your home makes you the happiest?

Would you rather have a pet armadillo,
a pet catfish or a pet cockroach?

If your pet could talk, what would it say?

What type of neighbors would you like to have?

Use two words to describe your bedroom.

If you could sleepwalk, where would you go?

If your fridge could only hold three foods,
what three foods would it hold?

What's the best thing
about being home?

Who makes the biggest mess in your house?

What's your favorite song to sing in the shower?

What time do you go to bed?

Would you rather have one hundred dollars
or no bedtime?

What's your favorite book to read at bedtime?

Your toothbrush is missing! Whose toothbrush
would you use?

The TV in your house is broken. What do you
and your family do instead of watching TV?

What room does your house not have that you wish it had?

Would you rather have a big party at your
house with all your friends or enjoy your
favorite activity with two of your friends?

Create Your Own Story:

Let's go to (PLACE)
with (PERSON).
I can't wait to (ACTIVITY) when we get there!
I will wear my special (CLOTHING) and bring my (ONE ITEM).
I hope they have (FAVORITE FOOD) to eat.
Phew, that made me tired.
Let's get to bed! We can read (FAVORITE BOOK),
and I'll fall asleep with my (FAVORITE STUFFED ANIMAL).
Tomorrow, when we wake up, we can go to (PLACE)!